A Moment for Teachers

self-care for busy teachers

101 free ways for teachers
to become more inspired,
peaceful, and confident
in 30 seconds

Alice Langholt, MJS

DEDICATION

I started teaching long before I acquired official certification. I taught for fun – directed plays, taught drama. I even taught Sunday School. I did this because I was terribly bored with my daily job in sales. Teaching was my chance to have a good time. It was my boyfriend (now husband), Evan, who knew me well enough to be able to see me completely and told me to get my teacher certification. I dedicate this book to him, in gratitude, for pushing me in the right direction.

Also, a special thank you to Ralph Belvedere, my student, friend, and a dedicated teacher, who suggested that I write this book. Ralph, thanks for being another person who nudged me in a direction that makes sense.

HOW TO USE THIS BOOK

You will need 30 seconds. That's all.

Start at the beginning, or turn to a random page. Every page has a title, a benefit, and simple directions. Read and complete the task on the page.

If you know that you are in the mood for a creative, confidence-boosting, stress-releasing, or peace-promoting task, use the Index at the back of the book to choose the one that fits your interest.

Notice the positive changes you go through because you took that 30 second break. Many of these tasks can also be shared with your students, allowing them to benefit too.

The changes you'll experience will last for far more than 30 seconds. You'll find yourself gaining more presence, patience, confidence and becoming much happier if you do this regularly. The energy in your classroom will positively change, and your students are sure to notice too. Using this book could become a wonderful little daily ritual.

By the way, the writing tasks have a blank page beside them for jotting your notes. This means that all you need for those is a pen. If there isn't a pen nearby, use a pencil. Even a broken crayon will work. You probably have plenty in your classroom. It's ok to write in the book. Later, when you read what you wrote, it will become part of your reflective process, displaying how you've grown.

Start the Year Right

At the start of the school year, instead of resolutions, make this short list:

- 3 qualities you want to keep
- 3 ways you want to grow
- 3 things you're ready to release

Tips:
- Try this alone or with your students.
- Review the list after the winter break.

Write your answers below: (Neatness doesn't count. Write and doodle all over the page if you feel like it.)

Ask Yourself

Breathe peacefully for 10 seconds and ask yourself:

On the last day of this school year, what do I want my greatest success to be?

Write down whatever comes to mind on the page to the right.

Read it.

Come back and review it whenever you feel like you need a reminder.

My Notes:

Say Affirmations

To realign yourself with positive energy, attract more good things into your life, and increase optimism, say each of these aloud and with feeling:

I connect with my students and support their growth.

I feel joy when my students succeed.

Each day is a new opportunity to make a difference in the lives of my students.

If You Could

Imagine that you are writing an anonymous letter to a newly hired teacher at your school. **What frank advice would you give to help the person be successful and acclimate quickly to the new position? Think of what you'd advise**.

Afterward, consider:
- What advice did you give that you wouldn't be able to tell someone in person?

- What advice would have helped you most back when you started?

- If you weren't giving the advice anonymously, how would you communicate the best of this advice in a positive and productive way?

- What parts of that advice would help YOU now?

Wisdom Break

Access and express some of your accumulated wisdom. Surprise! You're wise!

On the page to the right, write your answers to:

Three things I love about teaching

My Notes:

Celebrate Great Moments

Have a jar in your classroom. Whenever something memorable happens, write it on a small piece of paper and put it into the jar.

Students can be allowed to contribute too.

During the last week of school, or before winter break and again before summer break, read them with your students to reminisce and celebrate the year.

Just for Today

Sometimes, teachers can find their day taken up by the students who need a lot of attention and help.

Today, spend a few minutes talking with the student who seems to need the **least** attention. You'll make that student's day brighter.

Make a Success List

Do this for yourself on the next page, and keep a running list in your classroom too.

On a big piece of paper, write **"Successes"** as the heading. Each day, add to the list.

Even small things can make a difference. Let students put their names next to their accomplishments, and also include group ones. Completing a challenge, mastering a new concept, or even an act of kindness can make the list.

Review the list several times a year as it grows.

My Successes:

Energize Your Creativity

This is called the Cross March in Energy Medicine. It is used to connect the right and left brain activity, as well as stimulate creative thought and clarity. It's helpful for both students and adults.

For 30 seconds, march with your knees high, swinging the opposite arm and leg forward at the same time. So, when your left knee is up, your right elbow should be swinging forward.

After 30 seconds of doing the Cross March, relax for a bit and you will notice how great you feel.

Tip: Try this alone, or with
your students.

If You Could

Imagine you could be invisible and observe one of your students talking to his parents about his day.

What would he say? What would his parents say in response?

Imagine the whole scene in detail.

Afterward, consider:

- How did this exercise help you see things from this student's perspective, and what did you learn?

- How did it affect the way you feel about this student?

Ask Yourself

On the page to the right, write **5 qualities of an ideal student.**

Then, ask yourself which of these qualities **you** bring to the classroom.

What can you do to strengthen each of those qualities in yourself?

My Notes:

Say Affirmations

To realign yourself with positive energy, attract more good things into your life and increase optimism, say each of these aloud and with feeling:

I am innovative.

I tap into an unlimited flow of creativity.

My enthusiasm is contagious.

Just for Today

No interrupting. Let those who speak to you be fully heard. Don't craft your response while listening, but instead, be fully present while they are speaking.

Notice how this changes your interactions.

Wisdom Break

Access and express some of your accumulated wisdom. Surprise! You're wise!

On the page to the right, write your answers to:

3 things I've learned about helping students succeed.

My Notes:

Strike a Pose

Research shows that your posture affects your confidence and how you are perceived. Striking a confident pose reduces stress and increases testosterone, a confidence-boosting hormone in the male and female bodies.

For 30 seconds, stand like a super hero - chest out, hands on your hips!

Bring that super hero feeling into your day!

Tip: Have your students do this before a test. After the test, ask them how it made them feel.

30 Second Meditation

Try this alone or with your students for a powerful effect.

Quiet your breathing and sit still for 30 seconds. Try to hear, feel and experience your heart beating.

Notice the way it affects you and your students.

Create Your Own Affirmations

Our self-image comes from how we define ourselves.

Take 3 sticky notes. On the BOTTOM of each, write an adjective that could fit into: "I want to be more _____." For example, "Productive," "Effective," or "Happy." Write a different word in the center of each paper. (Do not write the words, "I want to be more" before the adjective).

Then, above those words, write, "I am".

Post these notes around your desk where you can see them easily.

Tip: Try this activity with your students.

Refresh Your Mind

Fresh air and a change of scenery can clear your mind, wake you up and freshen your perspective.

Use this 30 seconds (longer if you can) to go outside.

Walk around, breathe deeply and become reacquainted with the beautiful world.

Breathe in Sync

Mindful breathing can relieve stress and increase mental clarity for yourself and your students.

Try this: Use the website Do As One www.doasone.com to breathe in sync with people around the world.

Try it for 30 seconds with your students, or when you need to reset and focus.

Suggested times: after lunch, at the end of the day, or before a test.

Invite Flashes of Insight

Think of what you would call your three "Best Ideas Ever."

Ask yourself:

1. When did you realize this was a great idea? Was it beforehand? In the moment? In retrospect? Or, was it only when someone else told you it was?

2. Consider your moments of realization. What were you doing when the ideas came to you?

What can you do to invite more flashes of insight into your life?

Ask Yourself

Breathe for 10 seconds, and ask yourself:

What did I love about my favorite teacher when I was a student?

Write down whatever comes to mind on the page to the right.

Read it.

Come back and review it whenever you feel like you need a reminder.

My Notes:

Say Affirmations

To realign yourself with positive energy, attract more good things into your life, and increase optimism, say each of these aloud and with feeling:

My classroom is filled with positive energy.

I nurture the potential within my students.

I bring my best to the classroom every day.

If You Could

Imagine you could communicate telepathically (mind to mind) with your most challenging student.

Imagine that you can do this now. Think of a message you would most like to communicate from your mind to his or hers.

Afterward consider: What message did you choose to communicate, and why not tell this child directly?

Is anything holding you back from doing so, and if so, how can you remove the obstacle?

Wisdom Break

Access and express some of your accumulated wisdom. Surprise! You're wise!

On the page to the right, write your answers to:

3 qualities of an exceptional teacher.

My Notes:

Drum a Beat

Making a rhythm stimulates creativity and produces endorphins (feel-good hormones).

Either play a song or think of one in your head. Drum out the beat with your hands on the table, desk, chair, or your body. Add complexity. Get into it!

Tip: Try this alone or with your students. It's a great between-activities booster.

Just for Today

Whatever we place our attention on grows stronger.

For today, with that in mind, give the most attention to **positive thoughts, positive feelings, and gratitude**.

Notice how this changes your interactions in and out of the classroom.

Grow Yourself

Think of a teaching topic that you'd like to learn more about.

Look online to find a professional development workshop that addresses the topic you're interested in, whether online or in person, and make plans to attend.

Ongoing learning is energizing for teachers, and you can share what you learn with your colleagues.

Say, "What's Next?"

When problems arise, saying the two word question, **"What's next?"** can help you be objective about solving the problems and make the most positive and productive use of your time.

Try this, and teach it to your students.

Hug Yourself!

Self-appreciation is important for everyone's self-esteem, whatever their age. Hugging yourself feels good inside and out. It gently stretches your muscles, releasing arm and shoulder tension and relieving stress.

Wrap your arms around yourself and give your body a good squeeze! Stay in the position for 30 seconds. Remember to breathe!

Tip: Invite your students to try it too.

If You Could

Imagine you could know everything there is to know about teaching for 10 minutes. Then you would have to go back to knowing what you know now, but you could keep one piece of the perfect teaching knowledge with you.

Imagine the knowledge pouring in, filling you with everything you ever needed and will ever need to know. Now, choose the piece of expertise that you will bring back with you.

What did you choose to keep? Why?

What steps can you take now to start learning more about that aspect of teaching?

Ask Yourself

Breathe for 10 seconds, and ask yourself:

Which activities engage my students the most, and how can I incorporate them into more lessons?

Write down whatever comes to mind on the page to the right.

Read it.

Come back and review it whenever you feel like you need a reminder.

My Notes:

Say Affirmations

To realign yourself with positive energy, attract more good things into your life, and increase optimism, say each of these aloud and with feeling:

I am nurturing.

My students feel safe and ready to learn.

My classroom is a place of peace.

Just for Today

Have a day with **no complaining - starting now**.

Tip: Invite your students to take the challenge with you. (If you catch yourself complaining, quickly say something positive to neutralize the complaint.)

Wisdom Break

Access and express some of your accumulated wisdom. Surprise! You're wise!

On the page to the right, write your answers to:

3 places to find great lesson ideas.

My Notes:

Find the Diamond in the Coal Mine

Criticism and negative feedback can hurt, but they can also make for a good learning opportunity for self-improvement.

For these 30 seconds, think of the last bit of criticism you received, dismiss the negativity, and find a tip for improvement that you can use.

If you find nothing useful, give yourself a tip on how to dismiss empty negativity, take an assertive breath, and move on.

Nothing is Ordinary

This exercise is for changing your perspective.

Think of the most ordinary thing you can. Then look deeper into it. What is it? Where did it come from? How did it get to you? What's it made of? How does it function?

Look deeply. Can you see the innate complexity? A leaf. A plain piece of paper, the carpet on the floor. Everything is rich and complex in one way or another.

Now think of your life - your body's systems, your thoughts, emotions, experiences. All of it - a miracle in motion. Bask in this for a while.

Tip: Invite your students to use this exercise to better appreciate themselves and others.

Strengthen Your Relationships

Connect with the best in your relationships and improve them by sharing. Choose one person in your life - perhaps your partner, child, or best friend.

For the next 30 seconds, write as many of that person's positive qualities as you can.

Notice how good you feel about this person. Give the list to that person later.

Tip: Have your students try this.

Read a Beautiful Poem

Poetry is inspiring and uplifting. Read a poem to remind yourself of all the beauty in the world, to connect with the words that move you, and to beautify your day.

If you don't have a book of poetry on hand, surf over to www.poemhunter.com. It's a wonderful resource for poetry of all styles and subjects. You'll find poems suited for adults which are more mature, as well as poems suited for a younger audience.

Tip: Share a poem with your students to remind them at any time of the beauty of expressive language.

Say, "I Get to…"

Change your perspective on chores and opportunities by changing one word.

When people have something to do, they often say, "I have to…" (clean up, grade papers, finish this project, etc.)

Instead, say, "I **get** to…" You'll find that this one small word can completely change your attitude and the energy you put into it. This makes things feel like a privilege to do, rather than a burden.

Tip: Try this with your students.

Scout Smiles

Look for smiles. When you see
someone smile, smile too.

Notice how much happier you will
feel by turning your attention to
noticing the smiles around you.

Tip: Invite your students
to participate.

Wisdom Break

Access and express some of your
accumulated wisdom.
Surprise! You're wise!

On the page to the right, write
your answers to:

3 things I learned during
my first year of teaching.

My Notes:

Just for Today

Freshen your classroom by
changing or adding an inspiring or
decorative item.

Invite your students to notice
what's different.

Change is good for sparking
creativity, which affects your
classroom environment for the
better.

Say Affirmations

To realign yourself with positive energy, attract more good things into your life, and help increase optimism, say each of these aloud and with feeling:

I am patient with my students.

I listen for the messages hidden beneath my students' words.

I am sensitive to my students' needs.

Ask Yourself

Breathe for 10 seconds, and ask yourself:

What were the qualities of the teacher I liked <u>least</u> when I was a student?

Write down whatever comes to mind on the page to the right.
Read it.

Come back and review it whenever you feel like you need a reminder.

My Notes:

Just for Today

Use your sense of humor. Whenever something that normally ticks you off, irritates or annoys you happens, instead of feeling negative about it, choose to make a joke.

Try exclaiming, "Good one!" or "Well, there's something you don't see every day," instead of giving a negative reaction.

Notice how this approach changes the energy of the situation and helps resolve it faster.

Meet TED

Get inspired! TED talks are recorded inspirational and innovative lectures which are free and playable on demand.

In these 30 seconds, search up **TED Talks for Educators** and bookmark one to watch later this week.

Act "As if"

Change your day by changing how you act.

Our actions actually cause our feelings to respond. Think: **how would you act if you were having an awesome day?** Would you walk with a bounce in your step? Smile hugely? Greet people with a friendly "Hello"?

Make a conscious effort to do these things and notice how it changes how you feel - and your day.

Highlight the Meaning

A Harvard study showed that employees who feel that the work they do is meaningful are happier at work than those who don't.

Use these 30 seconds to list as many reasons as you can think of that prove your work as a teacher has a meaningful and positive impact. Write them all over this page.

After this exercise, notice the difference in how you feel.

30 Second Dance-Off

Dancing has been shown to release stress, increase flexibility, burn calories, and increase happiness (because it's fun!)

Take 30 seconds, put on a good song, and dance with your students! Enjoy the fun of dancing together!

Even 30 seconds are enough to energize and add positivity to your day.

Tip: Choose to do this activity at a time when the class needs a shift in mood.

Start a List

To stimulate creativity and inspire you, start a list in a notebook, on a piece of paper, or on poster board.

Add to it, review and revise it whenever you want.

Try one of these titles: Things I Want to Try, Books I Love, Cool Ideas, These Make Me Happy, Today I Learned...

Tip: Do this alone or with your class. This is a great individual activity or use it to make an interactive poster for the classroom.

Let it Go

Forgiveness helps us improve
confidence and move forward.

Put your hands on your heart.
Take a deep breath. Release.

Think of someone who wronged
you. Say or think, "I forgive you, I
can let this go now." Take a deep
breath and release.

Now, think of something you are
mad at yourself for. Say, "I forgive
myself, I can let this go now."
With another deep breath, release
it all.

Notice how much lighter you feel.

Stretch!

To keep the body and mind flexible, increase blood flow, and release muscle tension, do these for **5 seconds each:**

1. Reach up high on your tip toes.

2. Reach your hands over your head and behind you, looking upward.

3. Stretch forward, looking ahead.

4. Roll your shoulders forward in a circle 5 times, then 5 times backward.

5. Roll your head around twice in each direction.

6. Take a deep breath in, and exhale with an "ahhhhh!"

Tip: Try this alone or with your students.

Cash the Happiness Check

If happiness was the national currency, which parts of your work would make you rich?

Take 30 seconds to think about which activities make you the happiest.

Then, below, write three ways you can add more of that to your life on a daily basis.

Tip: Do this alone, or as a student activity.

Find the Fear

If a student has an outburst, chances are there is fear underlying the behavior.

Ask yourself what could have caused the fear, and then ask yourself how to respond from a place of compassion.

The answer that comes will show you the best way to respond.

Have a "No Schoolwork" Night

Every teacher needs a chance to recharge. Work-life balance is important, and it's easy to get consumed by the amount of work involved in your teaching.

Designate one night per week that will be for you and you only. That night, do whatever you want to do, but **do not do any school work**.

Being in balance yourself will make you more available for your students.

Thank Your Supporters

Office staff, cafeteria staff, and maintenance staff are all working hard behind the scenes to make sure you have a safe and clean working environment.

Today, be sure to express your thanks for everything they do. They'll appreciate it.

Ask Yourself

Sit quietly, breathe for ten seconds,
and ask yourself:

**What motivates me to learn
about new topics?**

**How can I bring these qualities
into my classroom?**

Write down whatever comes to
mind on the page to the right.

Read it.

Come back and review it whenever
you feel like you need a reminder.

My Notes:

Say Affirmations

To realign yourself with positive energy, attract more good things into your life, and increase optimism, say each of these aloud and with feeling:

I learn from every experience.

Every outcome reveals new opportunities.

I make a difference.

Just for Today

No using the word "can't" today.

Tip: Encourage your students to join you in this challenge.

Notice what changes (and point it out to your students too!)

Wisdom Break

Access and express some of your
accumulated wisdom.
Surprise! You're wise!

On the page to the right, write
your answers to:

3 lessons that fully
engaged my students

My Notes:

Wear Your Word of the Day

Think of a word that represents
what you want more of today.
Take a pen and write that word on
the inside of your forearm. You
can choose whether or not it will
be visible to others. **The energy
of that word is yours today.**

Tip: Try this with your students!
Either choose a class word of the
day, or let everyone choose their
own. (Use stickers if writing
directly on the body is
discouraged.)

Make a Growth Chart

The most accurate way of measuring growth and progress is to compare you to yourself, rather than someone else you know, or who you imagine you "should be."

Think of where you were and what you were doing a year ago. Compare this to where you are now.

How much have you grown? What changes took place? How are you doing? Celebrate your accomplishments and progress now.

Tip: Invite your students to try this too!

Go to Your Happy Place

Use your power of imagination to
inspire you and lift your mood.

Close your eyes. Imagine a place
that you love, or create one in
your mind now. Put yourself
there. Make it as detailed as you
can. Enjoy being there, doing
whatever makes you the happiest.

After your little visit is over and
you open your eyes, remember
that you can come back to your
happy place whenever you want.

Select and Use Your Best

We all have great qualities, but
sometimes we forget to use them.
Let yours shine!

1. Pick one of your best qualities.

2. Say, "I'm great at _____!"

3. Find ways to use it today!

4. Bonus! Pick a different one
tomorrow and repeat!

Tip: Try this with your students!

Visit Your Childhood
Dreamer

Refresh the spirit of the youthful
dreamer in you.

Think back to when you were as
young as you can recall. What did you
want to be when you grew up? What
dreams did you have for the future?

Now think of your present life.
Which pieces of that past dream
stayed with you? Which did you
discard, and which would you like to
reclaim? What aspects of the dream
can you bring into your life right
now?

What aspects of your students'
dreams can you nurture in them?

Connect with Your Tribe

Everyone needs support. Identify three people who you consider friends or mentors. **This is your tribe.**

Know that you're not alone, and you are there for each other. Reach out to them by email, text, phone, or in person at the next opportunity.

Write an Acrostic Poem

Express your creative self and your perspective on teaching at this moment.

1. Notice the word "teaching" typed vertically on the page to the right.

2. Write a word or phrase that includes every letter and goes across horizontally that expresses your creative idea of what teaching is about. **Note:** The first letter doesn't necessarily need to be the first letter of the word that begins that line. You have complete creative license!

3. Put your initials on your work, and date it.

My Acrostic Poem:

T

E

A

C

H

I

N

G

You Are Global

Contemplate: Your clothing came
from a plant that someone else
planted, grew, harvested, treated,
colored and fashioned into fabric,
after which it was sewed, shipped
and finally sold to you.

Your coffee, tea, and food were
the result of a partnership
between people and the earth.
Give thanks to all.

With your students, try to trace
the "global path" of an item in
your classroom.

Say Affirmations

To realign yourself with positive energy, attract more good things into your life, and increase optimism, say each of these aloud and with feeling:

**I model high standards
of achievement.**

**I see mistakes as
opportunities
for growth.**

**I initiate "ah-ha!"
moments.**

Ask Yourself

Breathe for 10 seconds, and ask yourself:

If I were given the chance, what would I do to improve my school?

Write down whatever comes to mind on the page to the right.

Read it.

Come back and review it whenever you feel like you need a reminder.

My Notes:

Years from Now

Imagine yourself 10 years from now. You are sitting onstage in the school auditorium. In come all of the students from your past 10 years of teaching. They each come up to you individually, share what they are doing now, and how your teaching influenced their lives. You hug them in turn, proud of their success.

You're setting the foundation for this now, although you may not yet be aware of the impact you are having on their future lives.

Share Praise with Parents

Today, find a reason to contact **five** parents and tell them something good their child did today.

Be vigilant about sincerely finding something to report, and share it.

The parents will be thrilled, and you'll feel great too.

Wisdom Break

Access and express some of your accumulated wisdom. Surprise! You're wise!

On the page to the right, write your answers to:

3 silent ways to get the students' attention.

My Notes:

Just for Today

Use surprisingly descriptive language.

For example, to answer the question "How are you?" instead of a simple "Fine," use "Fantastic," "Wonderful", or "Fabulous." Make an effort to choose extra-expressive words today.

Tip: Encourage your students to participate and feel the creativity flow!

Cover the Two Essentials

Every student needs to feel **likeable** and **capable.**

Today, do your best to make sure that every student is treated this way.

Set the Mood

Play soft classical music during quiet work time. It will bring a quiet mood to the room, and soften the emotional energy.

Other music types that work are yoga music or meditation tracks.

Say Affirmations

To realign yourself with positive energy, attract more goodness into your life, and increase optimism, say each of these aloud and with feeling:

I am confident in my abilities and intelligence.

I focus on solutions.

I am capable of handling all of my responsibilities.

Ask Yourself

Breathe for 10 seconds, and ask yourself:

If I were given the chance, how would I improve the education system in this country?

Write down whatever comes to mind on the page to the right. Read it.

Come back and review it whenever you feel like you need a reminder.

My Notes:

See the Best

Some of your students might present challenges to you. You will realize that they, themselves, are challenged at such times.

Though you might feel frustrated, you want to make a difference, advocate, and help your students have the best opportunity for success.

For these 30 seconds, think of one of those students, and write a list of that student's strongest qualities. Share that list with the student in private, so the student knows you notice him or her.

Repeat whenever needed.

Get Happy

Focusing on things that make you happy helps you feel happier, and you'll notice yourself having more of those happy moments throughout your day.

Right now, list three little moments that made you happy today. Was it the smell of coffee? The birds tweeting outside? A smile someone gave you? Nothing is too small to be counted.

Afterward, be ready to notice the next one when it happens.

Share Yourself

Your students want to know you better. Think of something new about yourself that you can tell your students today.

Suggestions: a hobby, special talent, favorite dessert, favorite song, childhood antic, or a good vacation memory.

Declutter Your Space

An organized work space helps the mind think more clearly.

In these 30 seconds, clear a space or reorganize something around you.

Notice the clarity of thought that follows.

Wisdom Break

Access and express some of your accumulated wisdom. Surprise! You're wise!

On the page to the right, write your answers to:

3 things I've learned about managing my time.

My Notes

Read for Fun

You encourage your students to read, yet when was the last time you read something for pleasure? Reading for fun is entertaining, enriching, and helps you become a more interesting and well-rounded person.

What do you like to read? Use these 30 seconds to go online to Amazon, Goodreads.com, or the library and search for something that interests you - and get it.

You'll feel excited to dig in!

Be a Safe Place

When you're a teacher, your students' problems become as important as your own. You empathize, worry, and constantly think about how to help them. It can become overwhelming.

Take a deep breath. All you really need to be is **safe.** Offer them a safe person to talk to, a safe place to be, and a safe place to express themselves.

That sets the foundation for everything else.

Make a Motto

In 30 seconds, you can come up with a motto for the day. It can be for you, or for your whole class. You can invite your students to suggest one.

Essentially, it's a positive and inspiring 3- or 4- word message.

Examples: Today I am brave! I can do hard things! I've got it, and I'm ready!

Pick it, say it, and let it carry your energy today.

If You Could

Imagine that you could be the Superintendent of Schools for one day.

- What kind of changes would you make?

- What messages would you want to share?

- What can you do as a teacher to help move your school toward positive changes?

Ask Yourself

Sit quietly, breathe for ten seconds, and ask yourself:

What would I most like to tell the parents of my students?

Write down whatever comes to mind on the page to the right.

Read it.

Come back and review it whenever you feel like you need a reminder.

My Notes:

Say Affirmations

To realign yourself with positive
energy, attract more good things
into your life, and increase
optimism, say each of these aloud
and with feeling:

I am approachable.

I will accomplish everything I need to today.

I am energized.

Refresh Your Classroom

Use this exercise to clean and infuse your classroom with good energy.

Close your eyes and imagine a great bright light that starts in the center of the room. See it grow bigger and brighter, expanding to fill the space. As it grows, any dark color and negative energy is instantly dissolved. Your space now shimmers with love and positivity. It surrounds you and all who enter.

Notice the way your classroom feels, and how your students respond afterward.

Wisdom Break

Access and express some of your accumulated wisdom. Surprise! You're wise!

On the page to the right, write your answers to:

3 reasons I became a teacher.

My Notes:

Having a Bad Day?

Sometimes, disrespectful students, belligerent parents, and hard-hitting administrative politics can get you down.

Take a deep breath and feel the reality of this statement: **you matter.**

Years from now, you will be remembered as one of the biggest influences in your students' lives. Take another deep breath. Pat yourself on the back.

Build Community

Each day, let a student tell the class something special about him or herself.

Give a prompt or allow the student to choose.

Suggestions: a hobby, special wish, talent, favorite food, favorite book or movie, or a favorite game.

Who Are You?

Being a teacher is part of what defines you.

Your other roles and those that you accept make up the rest.

For 30 seconds, list all the roles you have in society. For example, a parent, a woman, an artist, a writer, a runner, a cook, etc. You can add to or change this list in many ways.

Realize you are a versatile person with a full life. **Appreciate yourself!**

Expect Success

Start the day today asserting that your classroom is full of the best students in the school and treat them that way.

- What will change about the way you see them?

- What will change about the way they see themselves?

Ask Yourself

Breathe for 10 seconds, and ask
yourself:

What teacher in my school do I admire most, and how can I adopt some of that teacher's qualities in my own teaching?

Write down whatever comes to
mind on the page to the right.

Read it.

Come back and review it whenever
you feel like you need a reminder.

My Notes:

Say Affirmations

To realign yourself with positive energy, attract more good things into your life, and increase optimism, say each of these aloud and with feeling:

I communicate clearly with my colleagues and administrative staff.

I am open to new ideas.

I welcome collaboration.

Just for Today

Today, be the first person to say, "Hello," the first to encourage, to smile at your students or fellow staff, the first to help.

Offer your attention and notice how it elevates your day and that of those who receive it.

Ask Yourself

Sit quietly, breathe for ten seconds, and ask yourself:

What are my favorite things to do outside of school?

Write down whatever comes to mind on the page to the right.

Read it.

Come back and review it whenever you feel like you need a reminder.

My Notes:

Wisdom Break

Access and express some of your accumulated wisdom. Surprise! You're wise!

On the page to the right, write your answers to:

3 ways to make learning fun.

My Notes:

Reflect

Think back over the year.

Name your 5 favorite moments.
Write them on this page.

Tip: Try this alone, and then try
this with your students.

INDEX

ABOUT THE AUTHOR

Alice Langholt is a Reiki Master Teacher, the Executive Director of Reiki Awakening Academy School of Intuitive Development (ReikiAwakeningAcademy.com), and the founder of Practical Reiki, a strong, simple Reiki energy healing method.

She is the author of the award-winning book, *Practical Reiki for balance, well-being, and vibrant health, A guide to a strong, revolutionary energy healing method, The Practical Reiki Companion* workbook, and a deck of cards, Energy Healing Cards and app. Alice also authored the *A Moment for Me 365 Day Self Care Calendar for Busy People, A Moment for Mom, A Moment for Us,* and *A Moment for Success* (AMoment4Me.com).

Alice teaches holistic topics, and offers workshops on 30 second methods of self care online and in the Washington, DC area.

Alice lives with her husband and their four children in Gaithersburg, Maryland.

   Contact Alice by email at Alice@AMoment4Me.com.

Please review this book on Amazon.com or Goodreads.com.

Made in the USA
Las Vegas, NV
13 January 2023

65574217R00075